AF479872

Angry Bear Publishing House paperback edition May 2022.

For information about bulk purchases, please contact Angry Bear Publishing House via email at angrybearbooks@gmail.com

Interior Design by Lenisa Kelly
Illustrations by Lenisa Kelly

Manufactured in the United States of America

1 2022

ISBN 9798829404819

The information contained in this book *Let's Breathe*., is for entertainment and educational purposes only. It is not meant to replace professional medical advice, diagnosis, or treatment. Any attempt to diagnose and treat a medical condition should be done under the direction of a healthcare provider or physician. For any medical conditions, each individual is recommended to consult with a healthcare provider before using any information, idea, or products discussed. Neither the authors nor the publisher shall be liable or responsible for any loss or adverse effects allegedly arising from any information or suggestion in this book *Let's Breathe*. While every effort has been made to ensure the accuracy of the information presented, neither the authors nor the publisher assumes any responsibility for errors.

For my Grandparents.

a children's meditation book
for everyone

# Let's

# Breathe.


by mother/daughter authors

Lenisa Kelly & Lola Rand



Angry Bear Publishing House


Book 2

Start by placing your finger on the dot.

Follow the instruction as you trace the **Black** line.

End at the dot.

Turn the page.

Ready?

Okay.

Let's Breathe.

Breathe in.

Hold.

Next page.

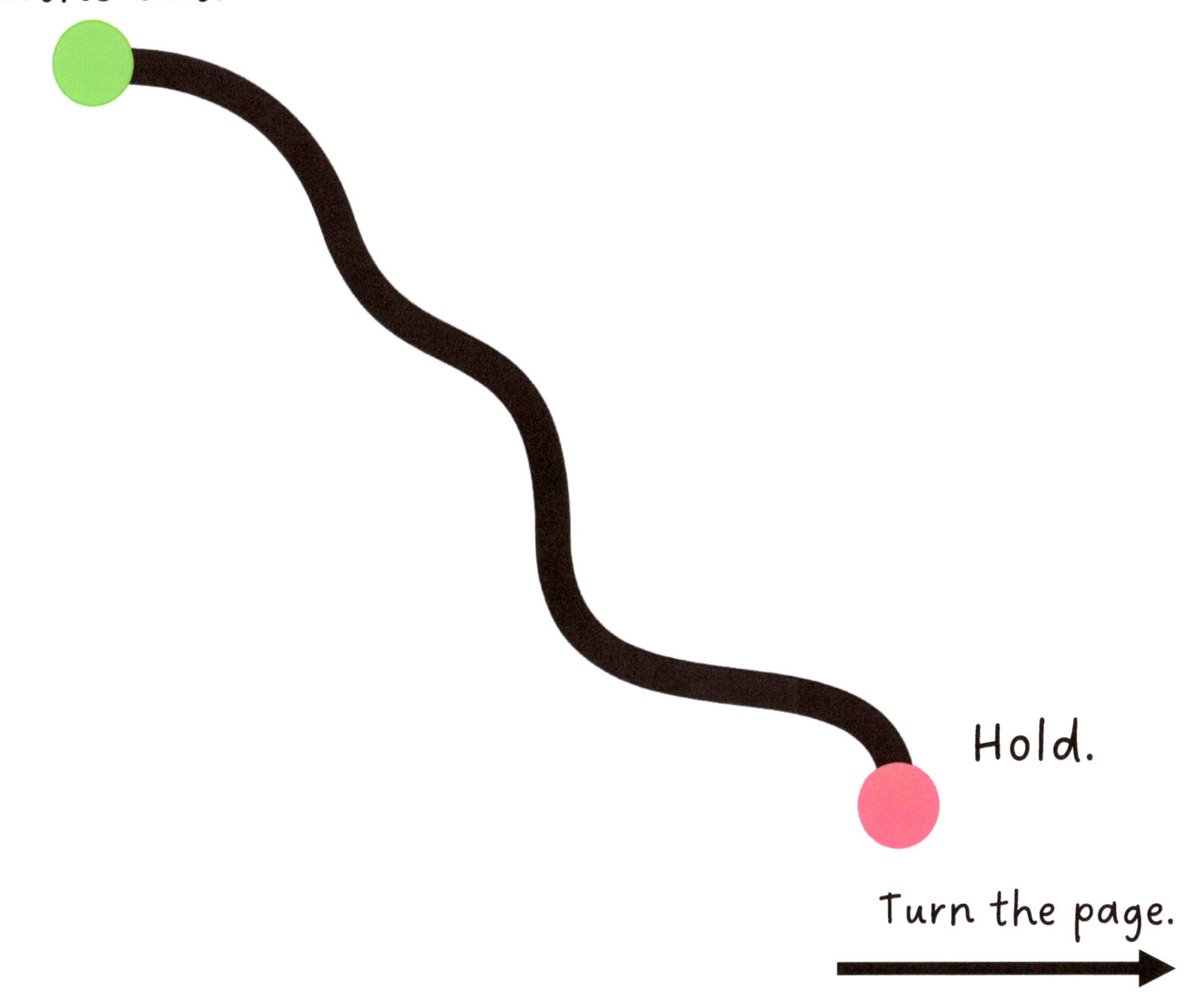
Breathe out.
Hold.
Turn the page.

Next page.

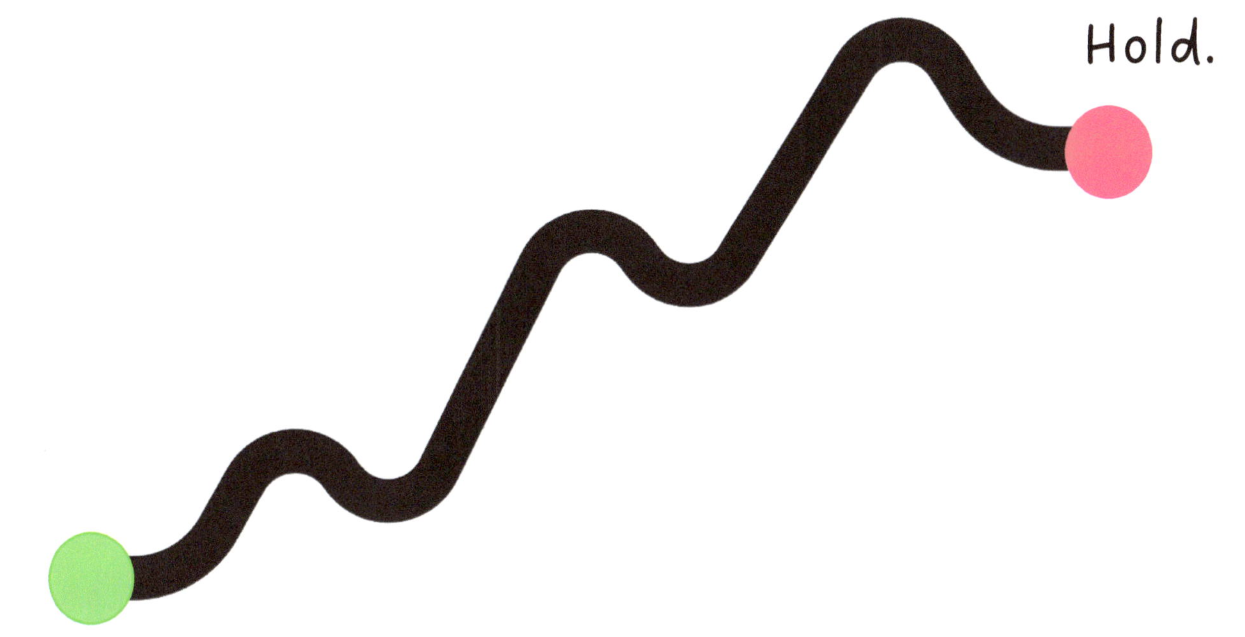


Breathe out.

Turn the page.

Breathe in.

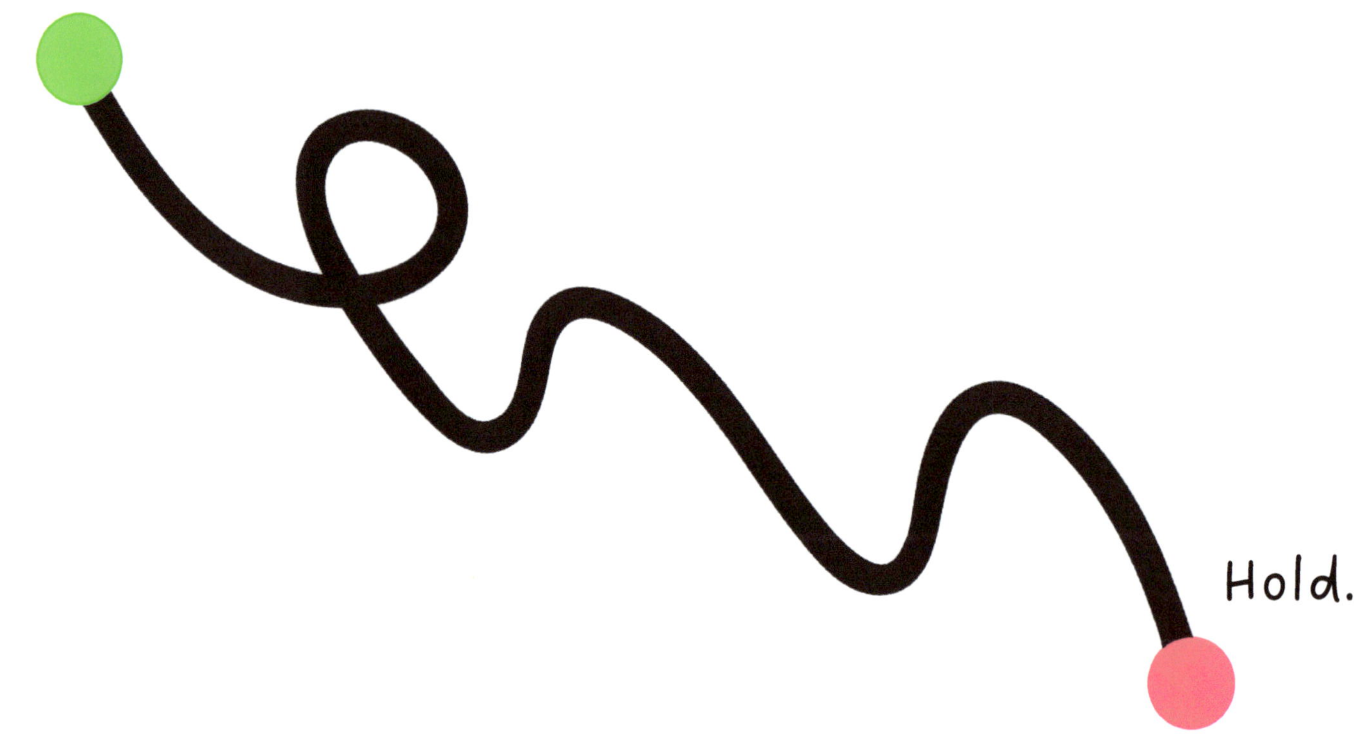

Hold.

Next page.

Turn the page.

Breathe in.

Hold.

Breathe out.

Hold.

Next page.

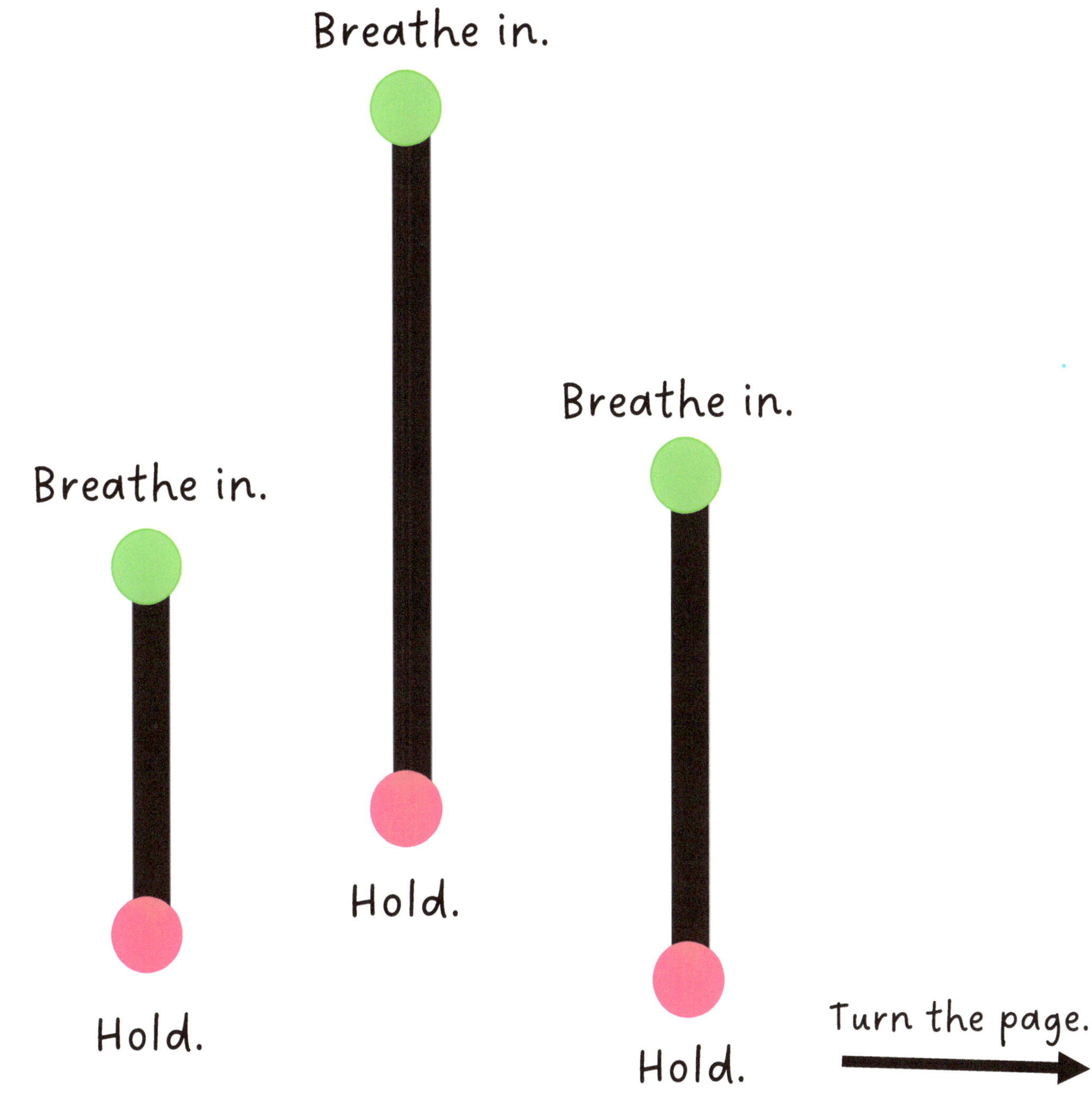
Breathe in.
Breathe in.
Breathe in.
Hold.
Hold.
Hold.
Turn the page.

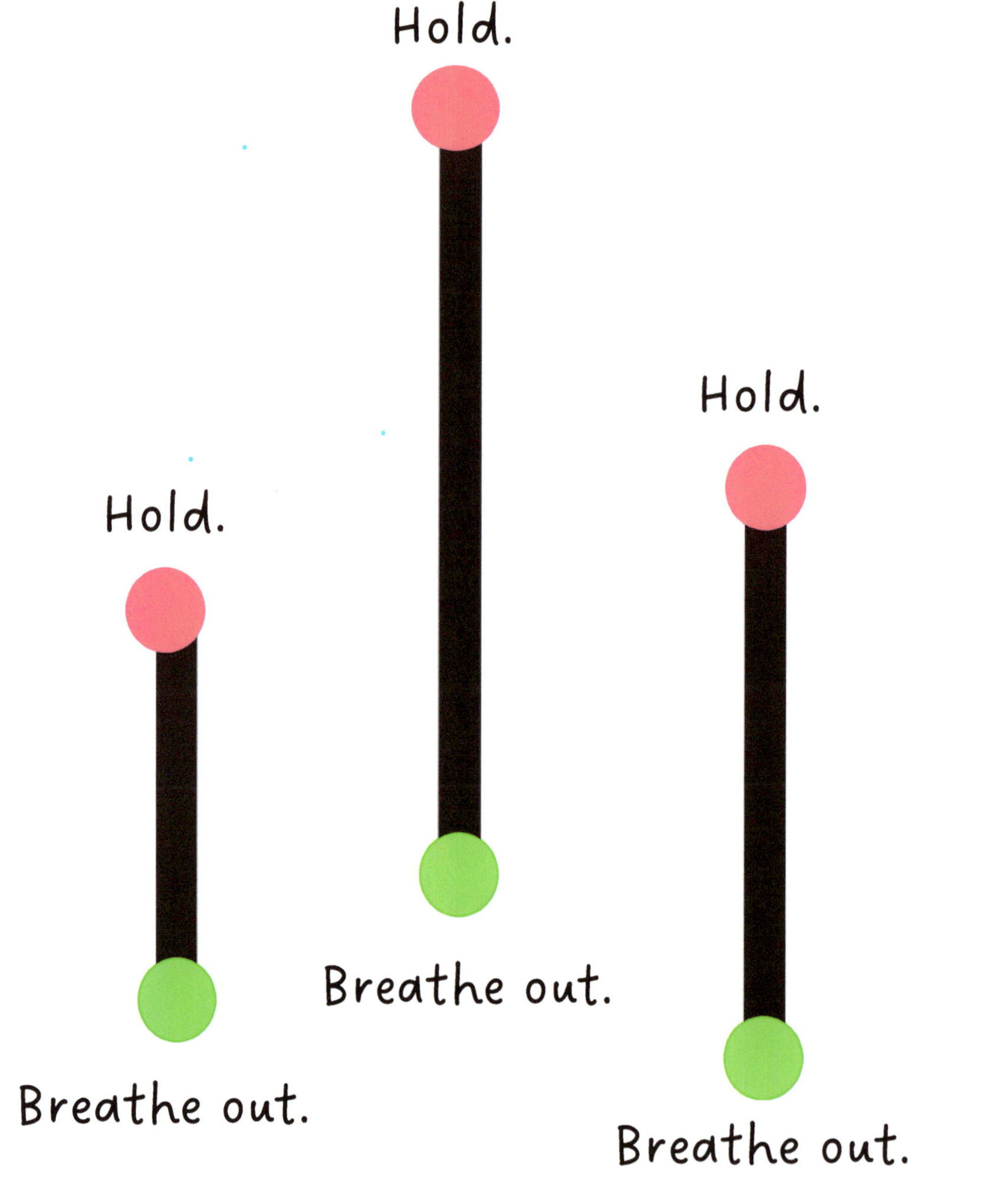


Next page.

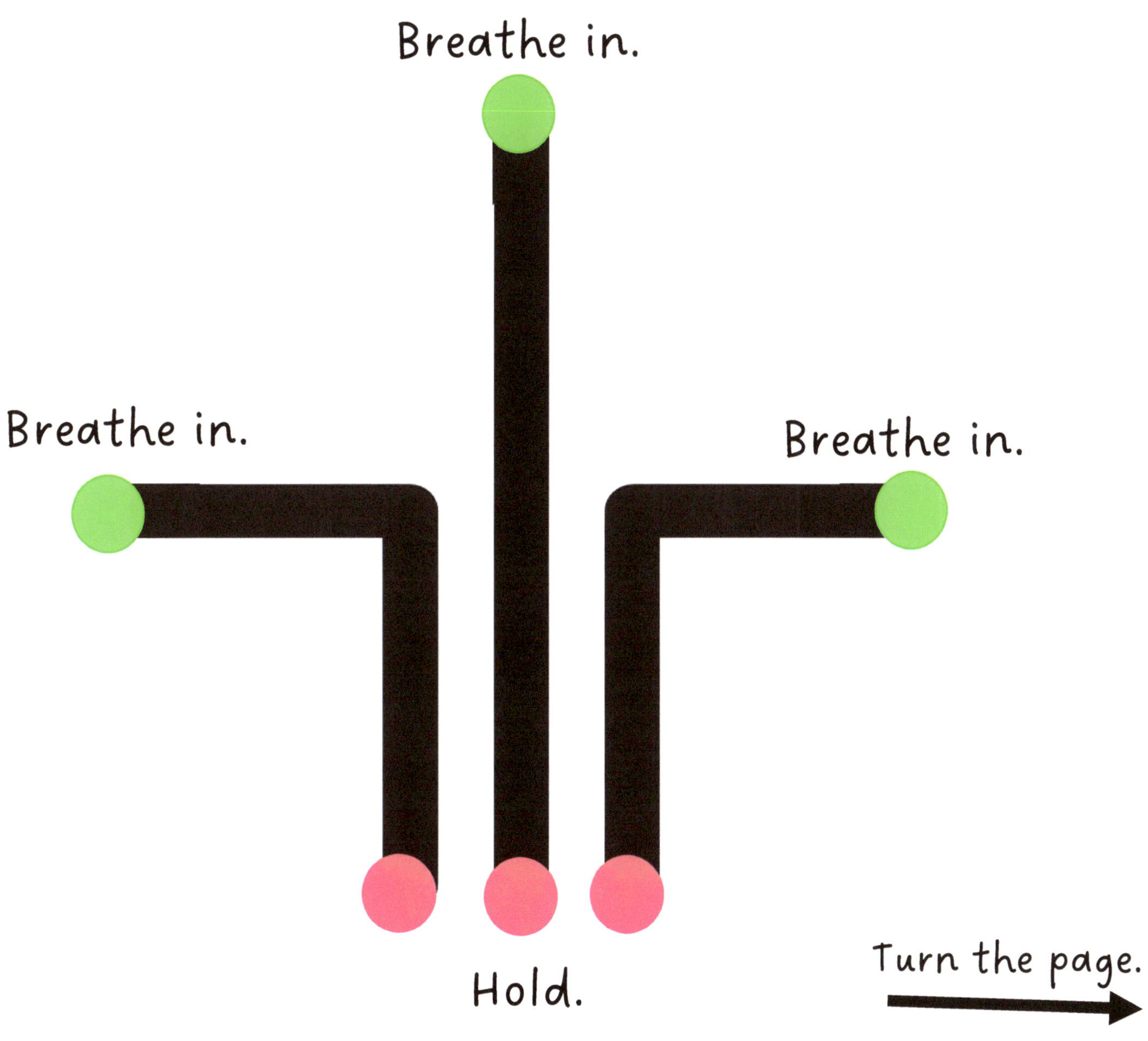


Turn the page.

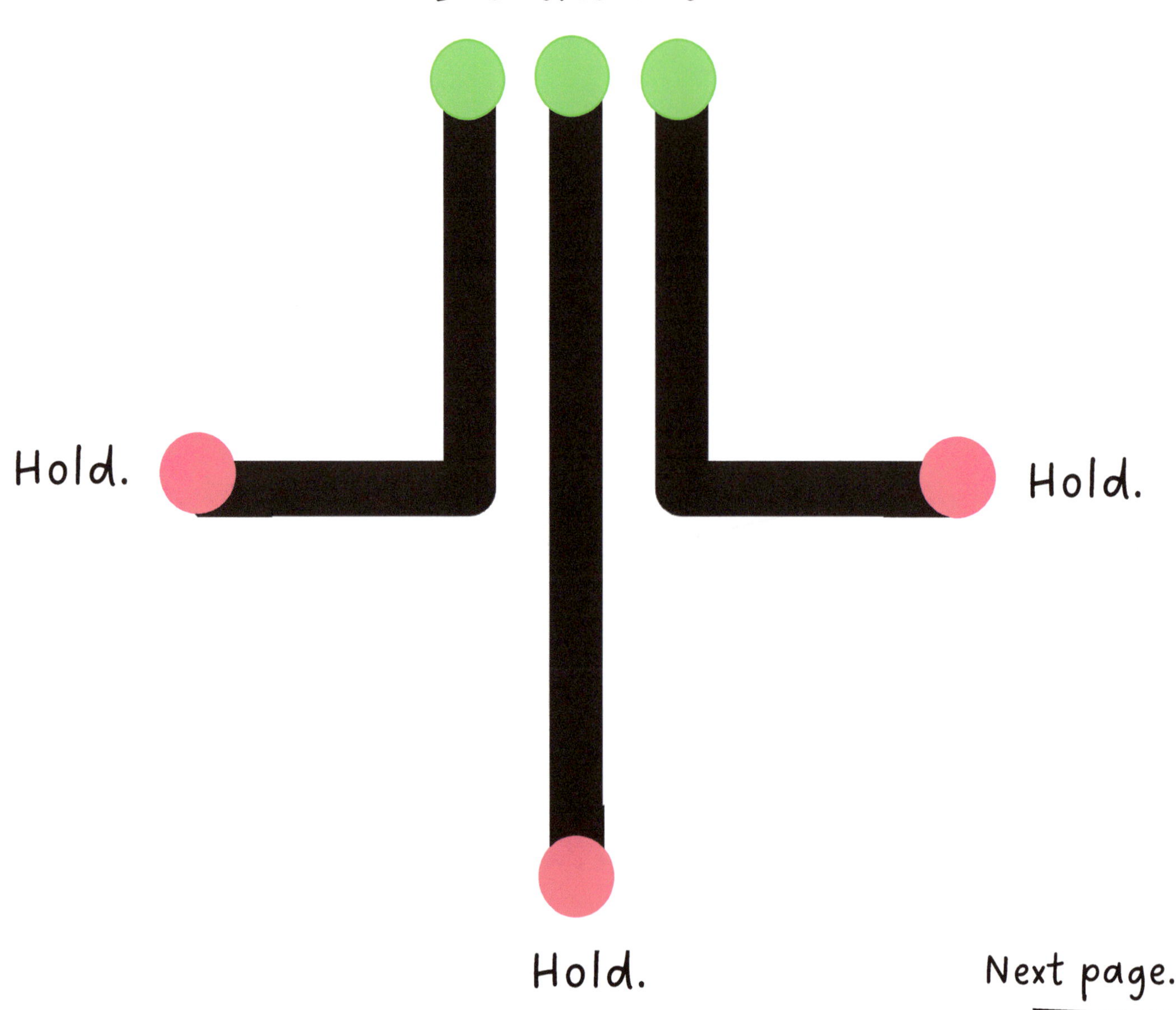


Next page.

Turn the page.

Breathe in.

Hold.

Breathe out.

Hold.

Breathe in.

Hold.

Next page.

Breathe out.
Hold.
Breathe out.
Hold.
Breathe in.
Hold.
Turn the page.

Breathe in.

Hold.

Hold.

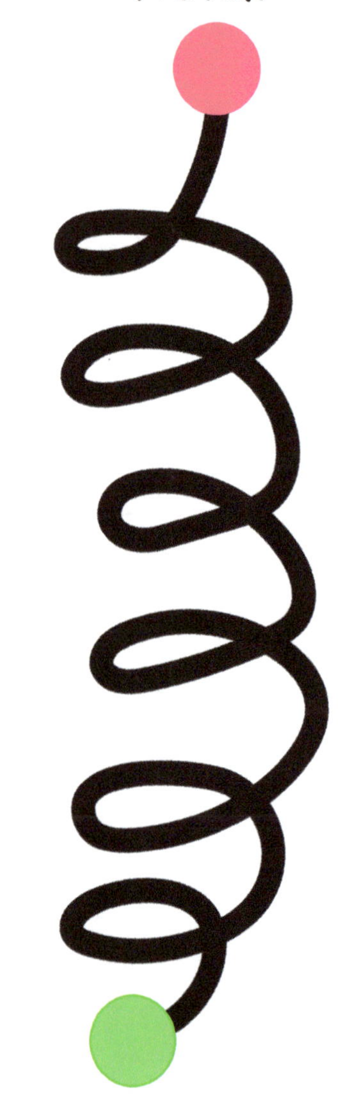

Breathe out.

Next page.

Last one.
It's a big one.
Get Ready!

Turn the page.

Hold.

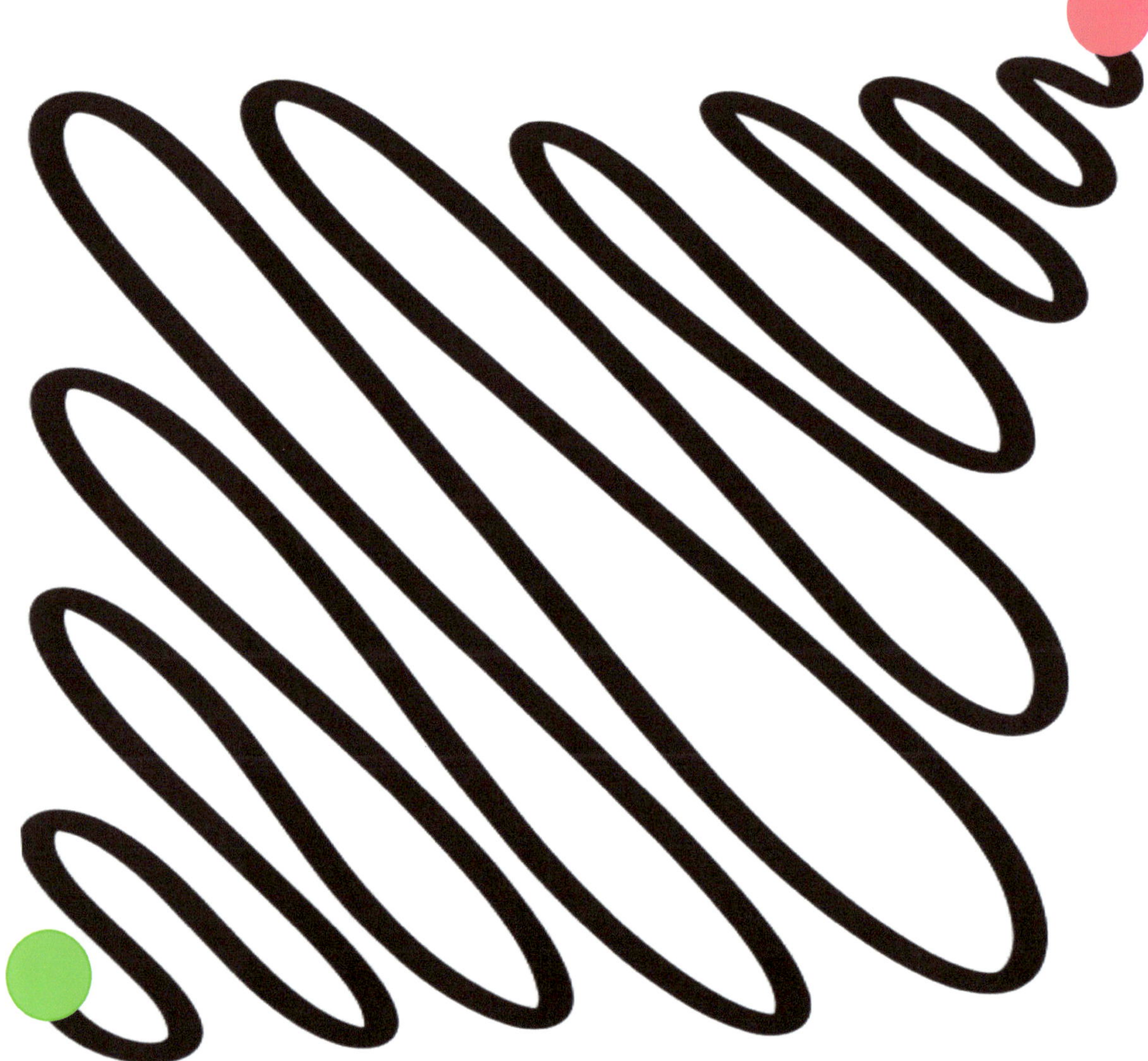

Breathe in.

Next page.

Breathe out.

Turn the page.

All done. Great job.

# About the Authors

Lenisa Kelly is a published author with a lifelong love of writing that she's passed down to her energetic, and eternally curious daughter, Lola Rand. This is their second children's book of their series, *Let's* Breathe, but certainly not their last.

Make sure to continue your breathing with our other books:

Available only on Amazon.com

www.ingramcontent.com/pod-product-compliance
Lightning Source LLC
Chambersburg PA
CBHW042115110726
48006CB00002B/641

* 9 7 9 8 8 2 9 4 0 4 8 1 9 *